Setting the scene

When you think of holidays, you probably think of somewhere with sandy beaches, blue skies and warm weather. But would you ever think about travelling to one of the coldest places on Earth? This book will give you all the information you'll need to survive if you decide to join a long list of brave explorers and venture out into the cold, icy world of Antarctica.

Reading investigation

- Would you like to visit Antarctica, or even stay there for a long period of time?
- How do you think people manage to get food in Antarctica?
- Which animals might you find?

Chapter 1
Into the Wild

First off, this isn't a book about the biggest icebergs and the fattest penguins and all those other incredible facts. This is a book about how to travel, dress, eat and survive in Antarctica.

Just you and nine-tenths of the world's ice in a single place.

Antarctica is magical but deadly. Explorers have been fascinated by it for hundreds of years. But why do they want to trek across it? There's no buried treasure there.

Why? Because in a world full of comfortable things – duvets and warm houses and sleek, fast cars – it's one of the last great challenges of human strength and endurance.

There are important differences between Antarctica and the United Kingdom you need to know before you go.

	Antarctica	**United Kingdom**
Wind	The winds can reach up to 200 mph	Storm force winds can reach 100 mph
Temperature	Temperatures are mostly below freezing. At the South Pole it's usually between −28 °C and −59 °C	The average temperature is around 13 °C
Rainfall	Antarctica is officially a desert due to low rainfall (average 16.6 cm per year)	The UK is definitely not a desert! An average of around 110–150 cm of rain falls each year
Sunshine	The hole in the ozone layer lies above Antarctica, meaning that the risk of sunburn is extremely high	The UK gets an average of 62 days of sunshine per year

Landscape	Antarctica is the highest continent in the world and it's covered in ice. It's the shape of an upside-down bowl. A trek from the coast to the South Pole will be almost entirely uphill	There are a lot of different landscapes in the UK – hills, valleys and flat plains, but all are mainly ice-free
Distance	It's about 750 miles from the coast to the South Pole. Antarctica covers an area of 5.5 million square miles	It is around 840 miles from Land's End to John O'Groats – the two places furthest apart on mainland UK. The UK covers an area of 94,960 square miles
Facilities	Very limited	Roads, hospitals, schools, houses, toilets – to name a few

Antarctica is a place that has killed many people, and it could easily kill you.

Have you heard of Robert Falcon Scott and Roald Amundsen? In 1911 they raced each other to the South Pole. We'll hear more about them later, but the key fact is that Amundsen won the race and made it home. Scott and his team reached the South Pole second, then died in a frozen tent on an ice shelf, just 11 miles from a store of food and fuel.

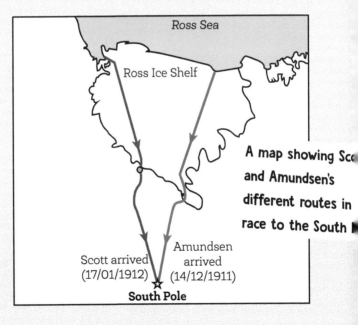

A map showing Sc
and Amundsen's
different routes in
race to the South

A few miles in Antarctica can be the difference between life and death.

On his way back from the South Pole, Scott and his men got caught in a blizzard and had to shelter in their tent for four days. Scott wrote in his journal: "We are getting weaker, and the end cannot be far. It seems a pity, but I do not think I can write more..."

And his review of the South Pole? "Great God! This is an awful place..."

Are you still keen on going? If so, you're going to need the right gear on the outside and on the inside. Clothes, food and shelter. Knowledge, physical strength and mental strength.

You're about to experience a world so white that sometimes you can't even see the horizon. Are you ready?

Quiz

Literal comprehension

Page 3 – Why are explorers fascinated by Antarctica?

Inferential comprehension

Page 7 – What kind of person do you need to be to make it across Antarctica?

Personal response

Pages 4–5 – Look at the table. What do you think would be the most important thing to take with you if you went to Antarctica?

Chapter 2
Clothing

The most constant danger in Antarctica is the cold temperature.

Body temperature

When it's healthy, your body has a stable core temperature (the temperature of your body's internal organs) of between 36.5 and 37.5 °C. Even really small changes in core temperature can harm you.

As you get colder, it gets harder to think and to control your body. If you can't use your fingers and legs very well, you're going to have trouble doing those everyday tasks you need for survival such as dressing yourself, preparing food, using tools and reaching shelter.

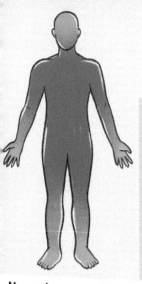

Normal core body temperature is around 37 °C

Hypothermia

If your core temperature goes lower than 35 °C it's really bad news – you'll begin to suffer from hypothermia. Even with only mild hypothermia, you'll struggle to take care of yourself. Unless there is someone else around who can help you, you'll die.

Frostbite

This is when your skin and the tissue underneath is damaged by low temperature. Don't confuse it with its baby cousin, frostnip, which is the red, burning skin you might have experienced on your fingertips after a snowball fight. Frostnip goes away when you warm up. Frostbite can kill off parts of your body – fingers, toes, or even your nose. Eventually, they go black and fall off.

A core body temperature less than 35 °C can lead to hypothermia and frostbite

Clothing

You might think the best thing to wear in Antarctica is a really thick coat, but the secret to keeping warm is wearing several layers, some of them very thin.

Layers of clothing trap warm air between them, meaning that you get to keep the heat made by your own body for longer. If you get hot, you can take a layer off so that you don't overheat and sweat. Sweat is not your friend in Antarctica – you don't need to cool down here.

When Scott and Amundsen were racing to the pole, their clothes were made of natural fabrics: wool, cotton and fur. Amundsen learned about what to wear in freezing temperatures from reindeer herders.

He used reindeer fur clothes to keep him warm, but not too warm. Scott did have reindeer fur boots, but most of his clothes were normal mountaineering gear from the time. These were fine for the Swiss Alps. They weren't enough for the Antarctic blizzards.

Today, outdoor adventurers can stay dry and warm using modern synthetic fabrics.

The clothing of an early Antarctic explorer

A person wearing modern clothing for Antarctic explorati

Which different features mentioned in this section can you spot?

The table shows some of the things you will need to pack. Don't forget to also pack plenty of mental strength. You're going to need it.

Clothing item	What it's for
Thin base layer	To wick away sweat, keeping you dry
Middle layers of clothing	To trap warm air. These layers need to be loose but not baggy
Windproof coat	To protect you from the icy wind
Thick boots	To keep your feet warm and guard against frostbite
Mittens and thin lining gloves	To keep your hands warm but also allow you to use your fingers when needed
Goggles or sunglasses	To protect your eyes. The glare from sunlight on white snow can be dazzling
Sun cream or face mask	To prevent sunburn. It's very easy to get sunburnt from the strong sunlight in Antarctica. You might prefer to wear a mask over your entire face.

Quiz

Literal comprehension

Pages 9–10 – What happens to your body
when your body temperature drops?

Inferential comprehension

Page 10 – Is it more dangerous to suffer from
hypothermia or frostbite?

Personal response

Page 13 – The writer says you should 'pack
plenty of mental strength. You're going to need
it.' What do you think this means?

Chapter 3
Food

Calories

In our comfortable, not-too-energetic lives we're often told that we shouldn't eat too much. An adult needs between 2000–2500 kilocalories (kcal) per day. A kcal is the amount of energy needed to raise the temperature of 1 kg of water by 1 °C. Growing teenagers might need more, around 3000 kcal per day.

You can easily double that for your Antarctic trek. You'll need at least 6000 kcal per day. The best thing you can do is to gain weight before you go. It's unlikely you'll still be overweight when it's time to come home.

What to eat

Survival often depends on knowing how to hunt and collect food wherever you are. Unfortunately, the wild foods in Antarctica are penguins and seals. Explorers used to eat them – in fact, Amundsen discovered that eating raw penguin meat was a good way to stay healthy. He also found that you could tempt penguins to come close to you if you played music to them! Of course, eating penguins is banned now.

Explorers also used to bring food in the form of live animals from home. Amundsen carefully planned his journey around this: his team used huskies to pull their sledges then gradually ate the huskies as they went along. Scott took ponies but he didn't want to eat them. We know what happened to Scott.

Eating a high fat, high protein diet is the most successful way to stay healthy in Antarctica. This used to mean eating pemmican, a mixture of dried meat and fat that could be cooked up with snow to make 'hoosh', a meaty, fatty stew. It is eaten with dried ship's biscuits and not much else.

Fortunately, we now have dehydrated food. This is food that's had all the water taken out, which makes it lighter to carry. When you stop to eat, you'll gather snow, melt it, then use it to rehydrate your food again. Because dehydrated food stays edible for so much longer than fresh food, you'll be able to enjoy chicken curries, beef stews and mushroom risotto brought back to life by a small portable stove and the Antarctic snow.

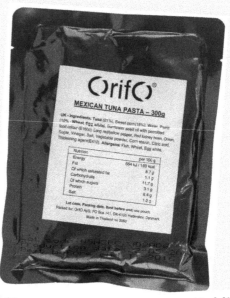

MEXICAN TUNA PASTA – 300g

A pouch of dehydrated food, like the kind that modern-day explorers might take to Antarctica

Meals won't get you to that 6000 kcal mark by themselves, though. You'll need to do some serious snacking. Chocolate? Plenty of that. Chocolate is one of the best ways of carrying around fat that you actually want to eat, and even when it freezes, it's still edible.

The diet of a modern explorer

Breakfast:

- porridge with powdered cream

Snacks:

- chocolate
- nuts
- cereal/seed bars
- dried meat (jerky)
- protein shakes

Dinner:

- rehydrated meal straight from the bag

What about fresh food, you ask? Forget it.

Explorers Ben Saunders and Tarka L'Herpiniere

Ben Saunders and Tarka L'Herpiniere trekked to the South Pole and back from the coast of Antarctica between 2013 and 2014, in memory of Scott's failed attempt. They took four months' worth of food.

It was packed into daily ration bags so that they knew they had exactly enough. Each sledge containing their food and gear weighed over 200 kg when they set off and they had to drag it all by hand. But, at least their sledges were much lighter on their way back!

Literal comprehension

Page 15 – How many kilocalories (kcal) does an Antarctic explorer need to eat every day?

Inferential comprehension

Page 19 – The writer says 'What about fresh food, you ask? Forget it.' Why would taking fresh food to Antarctica be a bad idea?

Personal response

Page 19 – Look again at the diet of a modern explorer. Which of these foods would you want to eat in Antarctica? Why?

What have we learned so far?

You have read about how different Antarctica and the UK really are – and how dangerous Antarctica can be. You have learned about the different types of clothing you'd need to take with you to protect you from the extreme temperatures, and the typical diet of an Antarctic explorer.

Question to consider

Which home comforts would you miss the most if you travelled to Antarctica?

Coming up next

You will read about shelter on Antarctica and different ways of travelling across the snowy landscape.

Chapter 4
Shelter

After a hard trek, you'll need to set up camp. We've seen the danger you can be in from the cold. You need to make sure that you've got enough protection from the elements to lie still for a few hours and still be alive at the end of it.

Bivvy bags

If the weather is mild, you might be able to 'bivvy' down in a plastic bivvy sack. This is basically a large plastic bag with a zip. Get inside and you'll be dry and warm for a while. You won't want to rely on one for your whole journey, though – remember, the wind picks up fast around here!

Sleeping bags

The days of reindeer fur sleeping bags are over. Explorers now use extremely thick sleeping bags made of synthetic fibres, developed specially for mountaineers. They might have extra pockets inside so that you can keep electrical things warm. When batteries get too cold they don't work well. This could be a real problem if you're using electronic equipment such as satellite phones.

Tents

Scott used canvas pyramid tents, which are still used by scientists in Antarctica. They are heavier than some tents you'd use at home (each weighs about 30 kg) but can withstand strong winds. They have a flap of fabric all the way round that lies flat on the ground and is piled with blocks of ice to anchor the tent down. They also have space in the middle for a person to stand up, which can be very welcome if you're stuck inside for days on end.

Canvas pyramid tents

Most explorers now use modern dome tents, which are much lighter. They need to be extremely strong to stand up against the winds – the one you use for camping in the garden won't make the grade.

When pitching your tent, you want to make sure the entrance faces across the wind. If the entrance faces into the wind, when you open the door, the wind will rush inside and take the tent away. If the entrance faces directly downwind it may get buried by drifting snow.

You can also saw blocks of ice from the ground and build a snow block wall as an extra windbreak – you'll definitely need this if you're using a dome tent.

Emergency shelters

Are you feeling cosy now? What if your tent breaks and a blizzard is coming?

It's time to build a quinzhee – a snow dome that you can make quickly and shelter inside. Basically, it's an igloo without the need to cut ice blocks and build walls.

- First, pile all your kit in a mound.
- Put a tarpaulin over the mound.
- Cover it with snow about 18 inches deep .
- Pat it down.
- After an hour or so, the snow will have frozen into a dome.
- Break through a section at the side (the side facing across the wind, remember) and pull out all your kit.
- You've made your very own snow house!

If you don't have time to make a quinzhee, there's a simpler way to shelter: dig a trench, put your skis and a tarpaulin across the top, then some snow on top of that. It'll be cramped, but it'll keep the wind off!

Quiz

Literal comprehension

Page 28 – What is a quinzhee?

Inferential comprehension

Page 26 – The writer says that a tent that you can stand up in would be 'very welcome if you're stuck inside for days on end'. Why might you be stuck inside your tent for a long time?

Personal response

Do you think you would sleep well on an Antarctic expedition? Why?

Chapter 5
How to Travel

Now you've worked out what to pack, the last thing remains to be decided – how are you going to carry it all?

Snowmobiles like these are commonly used to travel across Antarctica

Sledges

If you're trekking to the South Pole on your own feet
(plus skis), then the best way to carry your kit is on a
sledge. A hundred years ago, explorers used ponies
and huskies to pull their sledges. Unfortunately for
you, there are now rules which say animals cannot be
taken to Antarctica anymore.

There's only one thing that's going to be pulling that
sledge: you.

A tip: explorers sometimes attach sails to their sledges so they can use the power of the winds to help move their loads. When Justin Packshaw and Jamie Facer Childs travelled to the South Pole back in 2021, they sometimes used kites to pull themselves along. The fastest they travelled was 20 kph!

Bikes

It might not be the first vehicle you'd think of, but people have made trips across Antarctica by bike. In 2013, Maria Leijerstam became the first person to cycle to the South Pole from the edge of Antarctica. She cycled for 10 to 17 hours each day for 10 days with no rest days. Exhausting!

Machines

The scientists and field guides who work in Antarctica have modern machines to help them get around: snowmobiles, tractors, all-terrain vehicles, planes and helicopters. In Antarctica, you don't want the latest model of everything. It's more important that someone with basic mechanical skills can repair the machine if it breaks and that's more likely if it's an older model.

Roads

There are even some unpaved roads across the ice. A flagged route called the South Pole Traverse runs for 950 miles between McMurdo Station (the US base) and the Amundsen-Scott South Pole station. It was built by levelling snow and filling in crevasses. All routes in Antarctica need to be constantly checked, because new crevasses can open up in the ice at any time.

Navigating

You really don't want to get lost in Antarctica, but it's easy to do it – almost everything is white. Explorers used to use the angle of the sun and the positions of the stars to work out which direction they should be heading in. Fortunately, you'll be able to use Global Positioning System (GPS) technology, which uses satellites to tell you exactly where you are on the planet. It's not a bad idea to take some of the old explorers' knowledge with you, though – there's always a chance that modern technology might fail.

How to navigate using the sun:

- Face the direction you need to travel in (use a compass to work this out if you need to).
- Reach out your hand as if you were going to grab the sun.
- Stay like that for a couple of seconds so you remember the angle your arm is from your body.
- Lower your arm and walk on, keeping the sun in the same place.
- Repeat this every 10 minutes as the sun moves across the sky.

If the sun is behind you, then reach out along your shadow instead.

Quiz

Literal comprehension

Page 35 – Why is it so easy to get lost in Antarctica?

Inferential comprehension

Page 33 – Why is a bike a surprising choice of vehicle for travelling across the Antarctic?

Personal response

How would you choose to travel across Antarctica? Why?

Chapter 6
Getting There

The seasons

First things first: the seasons in the Southern Hemisphere are the opposite way round to the Northern Hemisphere, where Europe is. Midsummer's Day, 21 June, is actually Midwinter's Day in Antarctica. Also, you can forget about crisp, bright winter's days – the winters in Antarctica are dark! Right at the South Pole, the sun rises above the horizon for six months, then dips below it for the next six. So there is no proper daylight for six months!

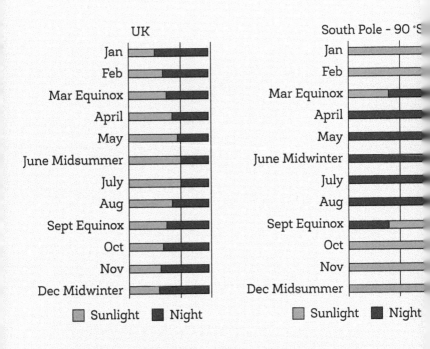

These graphs show how days in the UK always have a mix of daylight and nighttime - longer days in the summer, and longer nights in the winter. But in Antarctica, some months have full 24-hour days of daylight, while in other months it looks like nighttime all day long!

If you want to actually see anything (and not freeze to death), you'd better travel there in the Antarctic summer.

The frozen seas

It's not plain sailing to get to Antarctica. The Drake Passage between the tip of South America and Antarctica is one of the roughest stretches of sea in the world, with waves up to 7 metres high. Other routes go from New Zealand across to the Ross Sea.

If you time things well (and have luck on your side), you'll get to Antarctica when there isn't much pack ice – that's the floating ice around the continent. Pack ice can crush the hull of a ship, so ships sailing to Antarctica need to have reinforced hulls to break the ice.

Ernest Shackleton was an explorer who tried to be the first to cross Antarctica from coast to coast. When he set off in 1914, he was warned by whalers at the whaling station on South Georgia that it was a cold year, but he continued with his quest.

When the pack ice melted late in 1914, Shackleton and his crew set sail on his ship, *Endurance*. Unfortunately, the ice began to refreeze again much earlier than usual in January 1915 and *Endurance* got stuck in the pack ice. The ship did have a reinforced hull, but that wasn't strong enough to stop the pack ice from crushing it and it eventually broke up and sank in September 1915.

Shackleton and his team were stranded on floating ice, eating penguins and seals to survive. They pulled their lifeboats across the ice, then sailed to the closest land: Elephant Island. They knew they wouldn't be rescued from Elephant Island, so Shackleton and five other men sailed another 800 miles in a lifeboat called *James Caird*.

These six men finally landed on South Georgia, where they scaled mountains and glaciers to reach the safety of the Stromness whaling station. After that, they arranged for a different ship to return to Elephant Island and rescue their crewmates.

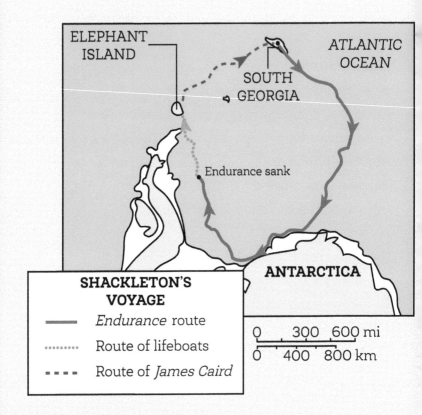

ELEPHANT ISLAND

ATLANTIC OCEAN

SOUTH GEORGIA

Endurance sank

ANTARCTICA

SHACKLETON'S VOYAGE

——— *Endurance* route

·········· Route of lifeboats

- - - - Route of *James Caird*

0   300   600 mi

0   400   800 km

Beyond the ice

Modern ships are tougher than 100 years ago and radios are much more reliable, so hopefully you'll reach land safely. As you travel closer to Antarctica, you'll start to see icebergs. There'll almost certainly be some whales surfacing to breathe in the sea. Whale populations in the Southern Ocean have increased since the hunting of whales was largely stopped, and there are humpback whales, fin whales, killer whales, minke whales and even some enormous blue whales to be seen if you're lucky.

Take a long moment to appreciate the stunning beauty of what is around you. A vital part of survival in Antarctica is keeping mentally strong. Allowing yourself to inhale a good dose of wonder and delight is going to help you in the hard times to come.

Quiz

Literal comprehension

Page 41 – Why do ships sailing to Antarctica have reinforced hulls?

Inferential comprehension

Pages 39–41 – Which is a better date to choose to get to Antarctica – 21 June or 21 December?

Personal response

Page 43 – Imagine you are a member of Shackleton's crew left stranded on Elephant Island. How would you feel? How would you pass the time?

What have we learned so far?

You have read about the different types of shelter on Antarctica, as well as the different ways of travelling. You nearly have all the information you need to make an expedition of your own – but maybe you aren't so keen anymore after reading about the difficult and dangerous journeys people have made to reach the icy continent!

Question to consider

How do you think you'd feel without daylight for six months in the Antarctic winter?

Coming up next

You will read about the animals you'll meet on your Antarctic journey and the dangers they bring. You will also find out about how you can live there long-term, if a short expedition isn't enough for you!

Chapter 7
Don't Feed the Animals

It's finally time to take your first steps onto the icy land of Antarctica. Take a really good look at your surroundings. You aren't the only living thing here. This place belongs to other creatures and you're in their space.

Penguins

Most famously, of course, there are the penguins. Five species of penguin live on the Antarctica mainland:

- Adelie
- Chinstrap
- Emperor
- Gentoo
- Macaroni.

Emperor penguin

Apart from having a quick peck or poo at you if they feel threatened, they won't do you much harm. Unlike Shackleton, you won't be using them to bulk out your diet. That's because it's illegal now to kill and eat penguins. The fact that they stink like dead fish might stop you anyway!

Seals

You might see six types of seal around Antarctica:

- Antarctic fur seals
- Crabeater seals
- Leopard seals
- Ross seals
- Southern elephant seals
- Weddell seals.

Don't be fooled into thinking that these chubby, clumsy-looking animals are slow or harmless. Up close, seals are big and keen on protecting themselves. Seals have a lot of bacteria in their mouths and their bites can cause horrible infections, including 'seal finger', where infection spreads from the bite and causes the bitten person's fingers to swell up.

All seals will bite you if they feel threatened, but leopard seals are the most aggressive. They eat penguins for breakfast and have been known to attack humans. In 2003, a snorkelling scientist drowned when a leopard seal dragged her underwater.

The best thing to do is stay away. You won't win a fight with a leopard seal. But if a fur seal comes after you, you might be able to persuade it to back off by tickling its whiskers with a stick.

Birds

There are many seabirds in Antarctica for you to marvel at, including shearwaters, petrels, skuas and the wandering albatross. Beware if you stray close to a skua's nest – they will dive bomb any creature they see as a threat. Giant petrels are also known for their defensive tactics – if threatened, they projectile vomit to deter predators. Again, staying clear is the most sensible approach.

One of the most amazing birds you might see in Antarctica is the wandering albatross. It has the largest wingspan of any bird on Earth, reaching up to 3.5 metres. It can also fly around the entire Southern Ocean three times in a year. That's more than 75,000 miles!

The landscape

A lot of the landscape in Antarctica is desolate and strange. Besides the glaciers, Antarctica has one of the world's most active volcanoes, Mount Erebus. A huge plume of blood-red saltwater, known as Blood Falls, flows from Taylor Glacier. Around 45,000 meteorites have been found here. That's two-thirds of all the meteorites ever found on Earth.

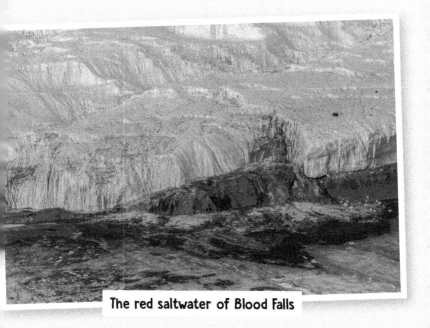

The red saltwater of Blood Falls

You will also see sastrugi. This is where the snow is in hard ridges. If you hit them, your sledge might tip over: this happened to the explorer Preet Chandi. But Preet eventually completed the longest solo trek by a woman of colour in January 2023.

She said, "I don't just want to break the glass ceiling, I want to shatter it into a million pieces."

That's the kind of mental toughness and determination you're going to need.

Quiz

Literal comprehension

Page 49 – Why should you not try to catch and cook a penguin in Antarctica?

Inferential comprehension

Page 53 – Why is the water flowing from Taylor Glacier known as Blood Falls?

Personal response

This chapter describes some fascinating things you might see in Antarctica. What would you most like to see if you went on an expedition to Antarctica?

Chapter 8
Travelling Dangerously

You've got your kit together, you've crossed the wildest seas in the world and you've kept well away from the seals. You've got your skis on and you've harnessed up your sledge. It's time to get going on that trek.

Crevasses

One of the biggest dangers when travelling by any method in Antarctica is running into a crevasse. These are huge cracks in glaciers that can be very shallow... or can fall for hundreds of metres.

The danger is that often you can't see crevasses from the ground because they are covered with a thin cap of ice. One step forward and – crack – you're gone.

The explorer Douglas Mawson set off with two companions, Belgrave Ninnis and Xavier Mertz, to survey some glaciers in 1912. They faced the normal Antarctic challenges of snow blindness and having wounds that would not heal in the freezing conditions, but one day, Mawson looked behind him to discover that Ninnis, along with his sledge, had simply vanished.

When they went back to look for him, Mawson and Mertz saw the sledge about 45 metres down a crevasse, but they never saw Ninnis again. They realised he must have fallen in too.

Things went from bad to worse for Mawson and Mertz. Without Ninnis and his sledge of supplies, they had to eat their huskies to survive. Unfortunately, they didn't realise that husky liver contains toxins that are poisonous to humans. The poison affects the brain and Mertz went completely mad before he died, leaving Mawson the last man standing.

Alone and starving, with his skin falling off and his feet a mess of weeping blisters, Mawson fell into another crevasse. Fortunately, his sledge stayed wedged at the top and he was able to pull himself up by his harness.

A modern explorer using a similar technique to Mawson to pull themselves out of a crevasse

After this, he made himself a rope ladder which he fixed to his sledge. The next time he fell into a crevasse, it was a little easier to get himself out.

Mawson did eventually get back to his base camp, but his ship had already sailed away. Luckily, a few men had waited behind for him. Together, they spent the winter in Antarctica, helping Mawson to recover. They were all rescued the next spring and Mawson finally made it home.

How can you avoid falling into a crevasse? There's no certain way. As recently as 2016, people have died falling into them in Antarctica. Knowing how to get someone out might help you.

Whiteout

A whiteout is just that – everything is white. You can't see where the land ends and the sky begins. All the landmarks – the rocks and mountains – disappear. It's caused by light being blocked and scattered as it hits the ice crystals in falling snow.

The main danger of a whiteout is that without anything around you to help you work out where you are, you can quickly become lost. To train for Antarctic whiteouts, people put buckets on their heads and try walking.

If you find yourself in a whiteout, either wait until it has cleared or use your GPS or compass to navigate. Keep a very careful eye on it so you don't ever go too far in the wrong direction.

Quiz

Literal comprehension

Page 57 – Why is it difficult to spot a crevasse from the ground?

Inferential comprehension

Page 61 – Why is putting a bucket on your head an effective way to train for coping in a whiteout?

Personal response

The writer explains the danger of crevasses. How could you check if there is a crevasse in front of you *before* you step on it and disappear?

Chapter 9
You Want to Stay Longer?
Living on Antarctica

Ordinary jobs

Despite all this danger, there are plenty of people who
don't just want to visit Antarctica – they actually want
to live there for months or even years. And they can!
There are 99 scientific bases in Antarctica. People
live in 37 of them all year round. The population in
Antarctica is around 5000 in summer, reducing to
1100 in winter.

You don't even have to be a scientist to work there – there are plenty of other jobs. Here are just a few jobs advertised by the British Antarctic Survey:

- carpenter/builder
- chef
- electrical power generation technician
- electronics engineer
- field dive officer
- field guide
- joiner
- maintenance technicians – electrical and mechanical
- mobile plant mechanic/operator
- steel erector
- wintering IT assistant.

The post office on Antarctica at Port Lockroy

There are plenty of other jobs involved with keeping the bases running – caretakers, cleaners, shopkeepers and doctors are just as important in Antarctica as they are at home. There's even a post office at Port Lockroy which has a postmaster to deal with tourist post.

Extraordinary lives

Don't be fooled into thinking that an ordinary job in Antarctica is like an ordinary job anywhere else in the world. You're still thousands of miles from anywhere. Internet access is possible via satellite but you won't be spending hours gaming online or streaming content. If you're there over summer, there won't be much darkness, and if you're there over winter, there won't be much light. You'll be with the same team of people, day after day, so you won't even be alone that much, which can get frustrating.

People living on the bases for months on end do try to keep busy, often by being creative. They read books, watch films and practise yoga, form bands and even try to garden hydroponically (with plants' roots purely in water, not soil).

Mental challenges

Some people still go crazy. On the Russian base of Bellingshausen Station in 2018, a scientist called Sergei Savitsky was arrested after losing his temper and stabbing a fellow scientist. What had the other man done to annoy Savitsky so much? It's hard to know the truth, but one of the stories that came from the base is that the other man kept giving away the endings of the books Savitsky was reading.

This shows that if you're stuck on an Antarctic base for months on end, it might just be the little things that become very difficult to bear.

Has there ever actually been a murder on one of these bases? Again, the answer isn't clear. A scientist called Rodney Marks died in Antarctica in 2000. After his body was flown back home to New Zealand, it was found he had been poisoned. To this day, nobody knows whether this was an accident or whether someone had deliberately poisoned him.

Getting on with other people in Antarctica will be one of your biggest challenges. What if you get stuck in your tent for days on end while blizzards rage outside? Almost always, there will be you and one other person in a single tiny tent. Nothing is private, not even going to the toilet.

Do you fancy staying in Antarctica for a little bit longer?

Quiz

Literal comprehension

Pages 64–65 – You have to be a scientist if you want to live in Antarctica. True or false?

Inferential comprehension

Page 66 – The writer explains that, in Antarctica, some people grow plants hydroponically. What problems might you have, trying to grow plants in water there?

Personal response

Do you think you could cope with the challenges of living in Antarctica?

Chapter 10
Look Around You

Finally, you're on your way. You've gained a fair amount of knowledge about how to survive in Antarctica. A lot of the rest is going to depend on luck. We've heard a lot about things going wrong in Antarctica, and we've seen that even experienced, well-prepared people still sometimes end up in really bad situations. No matter how hard you try, you'll never get across Antarctica without some luck on your side.

Climate change

The weather is of key importance. This leads us on to climate change: the temperature of the world is changing, and as it changes, so does the weather.

We used to call it Global Warming. This is misleading, because although the planet as a whole is warming up, some parts of the world are actually becoming colder. One of those is East Antarctica.

While West Antarctica warms up and the ice melts, leading to rises in global sea level (remember that 90 per cent of the world's ice is currently in Antarctica), East Antarctica is becoming colder.

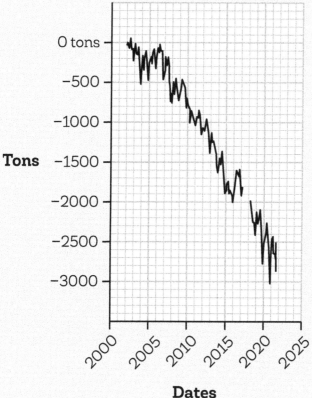

Antarctica ice mass loss

Tons

0 tons
−500
−1000
−1500
−2000
−2500
−3000

2000 2005 2010 2015 2020 2025

Dates

This graph shows how the mass of ice on
Antarctica has decreased over the last 20 years

What has climate change got to do with survival in Antarctica? Well, there are many reasons why it will change your journey. As the ice becomes less stable, more crevasses will open up. Animal populations might become hungrier and more dangerous if their usual food becomes more scarce. Blizzards might become more frequent, so there could be less time for you to travel safely over the ice.

Melting iceberg in Antarctic

How to survive climate change

This book is a manual, right? It's supposed to tell you how to survive these things. There are things you can do at home to help Antarctica survive, so that it's still waiting for you when you're ready to go on that trek.

- **Waste less**. This is an easy one. Use less of pretty much anything: water, plastic, cars, energy. Take quicker showers, take a water bottle and sandwich out with you, cycle or walk instead of going by car, mend broken things when you can, turn off lights. However small it seems, it all helps.

- **Raise your voice**: Youth movements across the world are shouting so loudly that governments have to listen. Future Antarctica belongs to you. Once the older generations are gone, it'll all be yours. Shout as loudly as you want, to protect your own world.
- **Do peaceful stuff**. Do you like creating art or music, making things with your hands, growing things, feeling the sun on your face? Do these things. One of the best ways we can all help the world is by finding peace in being creative and getting closer to the planet Earth, rather than shutting ourselves off from it and buying more and more things.

Antarctica tells us that the best method of survival is just that: to try and survive. There's a lot of doom and gloom spoken about the climate crisis, but the best way to approach it is likely to be with the mental toughness of Mawson, stuck out there in the Antarctic ice. We have to do whatever we can to survive, and there's every chance that we will.

A last word from Preet Chandi:

"Antarctica is not a place you conquer, it is a place you treat with respect."

Quiz

Literal comprehension

Page 71 – According to the writer, what is the one thing you will definitely need to help you get safely across Antarctica?

Inferential comprehension

Page 74 – Will climate change make Antarctica a safer place to visit or a more dangerous place to visit?

Personal response

What changes could you make to your life to be more environmentally friendly and give Antarctica a better chance of survival?

Published by Pearson Education Limited, 80 Strand, London, WC2R ORL.

www.pearsonschools.co.uk

Text © Pearson Education Limited 2023
Written by Ruth Hatfield
Project managed and edited by Just Content
Designed and typeset by PDQ Media
Original illustrations © Pearson Education Limited 2023
Illustrated by PDQ Media
Cover design and illustration by Collaborate Agency and Pearson Education Limited

First published 2023

26 25 24 23
10 9 8 7 6 5 4 3 2 1

British Library Cataloguing in Publication Data
A catalogue record for this book is available from the British Library

ISBN 9781292730523

Printed in the UK by Ashford Colour Press Ltd

Credits
The author and publisher would like to thank the following individuals and organisations for permission to reproduce photographs.

Photo credits:
Alamy Images: Arctos Images 3, studiomode 18, The Print Collector 32–33, Cavan Images 53; **Getty Images**: Daniel Milchev/The Image Bank 31, Cavan Images 57; **Pearson Education**: John Pallister 65; **Shutterstock**: Christopher Wood 1, Geoff Pugh 20–21, NaniP 22–23, Miranda L Miller 25, Philipp_Konietzko 26, Stu Shaw 34–35, TravelMediaProductions 41, sirtravelalot 46–47, KY CHO 49, Tarpan 51, Andrei Stepanov 54, Alexey Suloev 71, spatuletail 74, Goinyk Production 78.

Cover:
Shutterstock: Difught, Garsya, Katrien1, Memory Stockphoto, Nizar Salleh, Steve Allen.

Text credits:
Quotes by Robert Falcon Scott 7; Quotes by Preet Chandi 54, 78.

Note from the publisher
Pearson has robust editorial processes, including answer and fact checks, to ensure the accuracy of the content in this publication, and every effort is made to ensure this publication is free of errors. We are, however, only human, and occasionally errors do occur. Pearson is not liable for any misunderstandings that arise as a result of errors in this publication, but it is our priority to ensure that the content is accurate. If you spot an error, please do contact us at resourcescorrections@pearson.com so we can make sure it is corrected.